AF412541

RETURN OF THE WORLD

TODD BARON

O Books

The Rooms

we stuff machines or they stuff us
yet coming back to one body
that is really a gutter stream
from up the same block, some-
one washing or watering his car
was bald of course,
he had no hair & we being right
took what little comfort playing dead
in the upper reaches of a tree,
climbing thru a window to look for
something up there, up &
filled from side to side with music,
inside the room, was always dark, &
everyone's house was like that, no scheme
to the possibility that creation was all matter,
a boat somehow without lake, flying, above us,
no part yet to go to, it, being
nothing of the sort, we talk now, later
from an incomplete list brought about by some advent
that hasn't the time to
pluck itself from the book, to focus such
attention of the sound of this pronouncement,
careful in consideration, you might
smash the past with doctrine, making all time
an essay on syntax,
leaning to the remainders, a table, there, if broken
yields light, from where it can be seen,
down to where the action is, we had
nothing to speak of & yet were the lucky ones,
thinking, shouldn't they be the happiest children
on earth, the planet, resolves, a sound like
water, water like sound, over there,
behind spread fencing, topped at the top with razor,
who thought they'd improve the barbing-

if we indeed decree by moon or light
    "up-there" passing inherent
  to where it came from, gone
  as it were, in the passing phrase, back &
    once again, further on, where
  names withheld me, or
we fluttered by on the whiteness
    of nothing else,   late or passing
by, inherent in every-
    thing, we must have focused on
  the difficulties down, waiting for another bed,
thinking, a dug out place a hundred years later,
    a narrow bed a sea or lair
  withstanding the physical sense, satisfied, is
nothing left, late, about the space
    we turn over, then, if it is so,
  more space than time, no change
in everything actual, rings
at the bottom of a pool, head biting head,
  where the real flower sits
as it's known, splitting open.

something there that comes,
that comments on or will,
                    there by itself, grammar
of the field, field anywhere taken
where voice is fact of air, now that
seasons come over the bridge,   a man
woman or child, the act of stating "that's it", or
That is it.   sitting & reading, call it
Out on the Playing Field, a ball
held tightly by rope, the wrist, red, upper portions
of the plate,
                    place is a black substance, a rest
not a glottal, memory coherent with time
taken from him, linked to sleep &
language taken in seams, not by breath, a cool'd longing

what voice is mined, what voice is voiced, over
the drum humming,
by wanting
time & tone again, paper refolds
& is folding a secretive want
by the waves or the wants
fenced in the sentence's turning, in with an out
of a thick fingered now
light   light reflection, say
nothing, say self is bound
for circumference to stop,
temporality timed for collusion
where nothing heard
on hearing drops.

neither voice nor mention
to create the sound
    whose footsteps lead out
the door, whose footsteps are soft
    & dying, whose feet are remember'd
from here yet unfixed
    fixing them here,   no phoneme of
mention, no
word for the leaves
seed of other words

try to remember a thing, or
a thing doesn't remember me,
walks & talks & tries to,
air not clean enough, stance
really a sufferage worked by nature
to be still-born,
visible to emit
illuminating rays
to let the eye through,
a solid secondary root,   lawn or grass
or front lawn gets cut every week,
but wood softens, is soft,   what
need of sounds
to reciprocate,
form & rhyme to make
the spoken place
a placement,
it rains & doesn't rain, sun is
constantly up,
who walks a careful street,
a small & larger fire

            page a cipher word or script
           more than what is offered, only
      thought made up of mind, read-
               written
                      self-on-self, water-on-water,
            line or lines under
              bird or bird-song,
       though a name in my case wrecks things
             green & red parts, this
             shade of blue
         onto which a map is drawn: unfamiliar land
              to touch the ground
             whose voice describes the scene.
        takes things as a place of made-up timber,
             timed & geared to, running away.
   what does not fit is taken,   termed
           silence or stream, not
       conscious he says   he "remembers,"
        takes hold, which cannot
            give & take, cannot make
           by putting words in,
                          or if by pushing water
              up to tone again, shapes
              into a vacant lot,
             lines fade as
                 who is sung clings to the possibility
              of particulars also.

I want to write, and writing, write.
            so in the effusion,
deems, willow'd, branched,
comes a day. and there,
        here she says,
          moving in unmoving ways, chords so tight you fall be-
loved, into & out of
pith-syllable.   poverty of glance
              trees by a pin hole, someone coming
      takes this back from where it came,
    the text & the text, for texture,
      in tents not in caves, so in the final sense
    are other's language.   book on the table
    cup in the mask,
                    sun sticks in a circle of fire,
first rock or orb I thought would covet thee.   that I could love
          & love assuredly, heaping idols on the flame.
bloody flukes, despair & unbelief, that 'til my spirit
      rises, they raise.   sit, stare
    sighted, open in summer, to park, stare
    or place.

dancing from the cap
in the moment of silence, open
in the motion of greeting
ill-fated separation from the day, in the guise of
fabric, austere in the woods,
that I can find them
drinking from a mug of soap-water,
blue & grey
in a circuit of land, frozen sense
making sense-deprivation .

who, in the machine tree
at the bottom of a pool
      passing sight
   from narration,
                              unhinged
                  her voice
      as breath will be
      in the erasure, down &
          lifted "up"
       onward,
    is a film in which
      the bedroom is real but falling,
      where snow falls
      "upwards"
    at certain speeds
    timed for tuning what voice
above us, then
      to sleep
   which doesn't need of dream, also

or in the branching of something else,
facing a window
thru its own structure,
made of its own sympathy
by the focus of limbs
(intentions)
as are now yours   (mine)
burning an image, say
two or three stories at once,
then, in the passing phrase,
is it who or whom, made-up
in the upper reaches of speech
where it rains & doesn't rain,
this room and those rooms,
alive
to a particular place,
on the edge of a black and white set,
caught by a hook, going away
as syntax does not know
the words are not mine but written,
the words are not words, but lines.

Imaginary Song

single   trace
towards an imagined time,

worried that absence

leaving words discontinuous
rime

Away

*

where I was
in another place

&
where to
fall
to,

that an edge

makes
an island

& signs

at the gate.

*

for the birds in flight
by twos,   squawking

" a shiver of rain "

form

a species
somehow

to say, & said

but copy
a voice

this long.

*

to find a bit of rock
& call it "day"

whom "I" ply,

I watch you.

*

*

but is not
to sing

my shoulders

to hide my heart.

*

before me,

to catch the
eye

to sleep again.

*   *

nothing will feel
& is & is,

I have emptied
the morning

of multiplicity,

arching us more

on the pillow
towards us.

*

like wheels

the spring

with yellow leaves

coming full
from the fog

*   *

*

so that a well
between a well

to the trees,
falls.

*   *

to live
without question

the quote.

the real artifice

rides again
as he throws his

flame white disc
to the sun.

*   *

dear customer

you wrote a note,

it filled you,

all the changes mentioned

in quarter time,

& every penny to keep you, both

stable & table

will remain the same.

*

hence,
your
lips

with oil.

*

                *   *

to say & said
but to copy,

that an edge
might nest

to find you.

                *   *

<u>Imaginary Song</u>   *for Margy*

to retrieve   recognition

false shores,

sun &
all its
chores

inside,
"limiting the view"

any less "isolated
path of
certainly
not less
time, "

good   eyes
waking anew.

Axis

weight bowing
the body
is clarity,

only clarity, limiting
voice a
sentence ago.

<u>Pounding the Shore</u>

working in an old wound,
in plain sight,
in search of the simple life,
land of living rock
or car or bike,
where approaches to "where"
function at merely material.

elementary diary
blessed by light,
whose sudden artifice
is fiction,
scrambles out of the rock
or into the fire as
figures of speech watching
an echo.

he replies audibly enough,
"I can't, for the life of me,"
last time we spoke,
further & farther away,
as the year I was ending ended,
an education sour
by each particular note,
"this ocean, humiliating
in its disguises,
tougher than anything . . ."

anatomy of an illness
catapulted into space,
the present indicative
for a future indefinite,
the Great Stone Face.

"animated beings
grow old, never young,"
at the point of being
smother their causes,
the law of degradation
talking in my sleep,
clinging mechanically to dates.

the rain,   the wind,
off,   wet,
driving the play,
falling on a fallen day
singing   cheated
summer &
don't pray
without the turn to others.

an edible landscape
near the front of the drawer
the cassette
slips in.

zen & the art of repetition,
zen & the fall of the mountain,
zen & the birds of space.

"the celestial movements
blind to guesses,"
not yet awake,
touching the want of custom
the rope trick spells
"dictation".

if, in a wet season,
a number of acoustic phases
induces reason,   broken,
reflecting high decision,
regarded to discarded sentences,
approximated from the
cause diverted,
fully seeded,
all use evaded,
appearing ceases.

light that wavers
thinking of light,
between twin heads
seeking diction.

old enough to read

"see it
not break, but

see it imagine itself
breaking. "

the ash heap increases in size
but the mouths get bigger,
a state of order microscopic,
the sun smaller,
earth, colder,
moving towards a chair in the dark,
approaching headaches
at the end of day,
nothing added,
always lost,

talking in a room, taking in
a separation, 'bending the bow'
of consistent geography,
composing or decomposed.

in the place of an advent
the other voice said,   a house
a true   abbreviated tone,
but sees & hears   beyond doubt,
something later.

where the water goes
this is a notion
that makes this grow quicker,
the eye has it,
which verse is said to deliver, distanced
as if the anagram for something else
who does not know,

these cold spots
about an axis,
from one body to many,
unable to disengage
proportional reason,
a day's unceasing dispersion
of light
reflected sources,

to move
an averted gaze,
under the actions of
concurrent forces,

tension in the
inner workings
producing mass media
provoking change.

open the slightly spoiled
fruit of morning
whirled in horizontal planes,
mass pulls on
a wheel or
words missing
a letter,

to fly in concentric circles
syntactically from space
that a page tends to sound
an episode later.

inversion undoes
a projecting film,
visibility regains
an original face.

all these trees
& no water,

blue &
blue again

"pounding the shore,"

when a body falls
between us,

even the wind
to the door
keeps moving, even
in hands to my
wind to the door
of everything else.

*

So That

*

"what
without
days,

they
come
so much
slower,"

eat
of the fruit
I only
remember.

*

but if my light,
lost to the
senses
we pare, are

broken,
in the sun

alone, the

unknown
vocalization

of
these
flowers

*

Return of the World

at the tip of the container present
in this *me* in me, forgo italics
to find the letters which state
what they do not mean
in meaning it.
                  at the tip of the
present future, the letters do not mean
to find in finding "it"
which states,
                  alone in a bed of meaning
forgo the letters
which they do not mean present
what they do not mean in meaning it
at the tip, only

these are the formulations given.
once I step outside my room
at a certain age, this time
lost in another book,
the model of which
is broken.

take this time-bound heredity
the letters do not mean
in meaning the tip of
the container present
on the page in
formulations given
nothing of me,
nothing of me, nothing

in wanting to wake & waking it,
nothing but this day
which has at its cause
the smallest number,
                              letters not long
are the primary tools today
someone out this window
dead   at this moment
a siren proclaims   composition,
wanting & needing
to cause sleep,   language, dream
from the future its past
execution,   now the
time is   structurally long
surrendered in making words
somewhere

wanting & getting   fixtures
the mouth moves   either
truth or beauty   in view only
the t or b
withstanding   so meticulous
dispersion   neither house
nor home,   but the required place
of reference, while
crossing the street,
and the car itself
was crossing

removed from   sleep
my own words a
dream between fixtures, only
this view only withstanding
the wind   surrendered
its own execution, this moment
meaning   structurally
lost in the long pluralities.

the mouth an
island in, of
itself
          the floor's
reflection, dead
outside this window

does not mean
the formulations given
nothing of me,
nothing   crossing the street
which is broken,
now at the tip of the future
the bus crowded not verse only
poem my foot stems
in waking a bird not a bird
only   waiting, wanting & trying "it" which states
the future   italics

to find the letters
crushed in reflection
the light   moves
away from *me,*

once out of bed
& lost in it,
dream   neither house nor home
nor beauty not
truth & the lack of
faith in desire alone.

                        not verses nor
verses not
plates on the floor,
if in a reflection
my foot stems the longest poem
in waiting alone.

nothing of me nothing no
thing in the street but
crowded with verse not wanting

in/out
in other
motions of
meaning

            home
not,   get to a place alone, maybe
a bird not a bird maybe
a siren

only, shuffle the page,   forget
what meaning this window killed
is   an island   crossing the street, the
pluralities   lost
in the long shuffle   structurally
called from their own execution   wanting
a bird's silence a siren,

"it" is an island
moving away from me.
these are the formulations given.

a certain age
lost in another
container,   forgo
the letters   alone in a bed
at the tip only
at the tip only the letters
do not mean on the page
someone is killed,

nothing in front of me, no
thing waiting somewhere,
this wind either
t or b neither
home nor house
but the required sleep proclaiming sleep,
which has as its cause
the smallest number

surrendered in
crossing an island
at the tip only   lost
on the page in front of me,

what they do not find in a bed of street.
only a bird states
at the tip of the container present
in me, another book, broken,
the model of which is

a beautiful long composition outside my room
waiting & wanting a certain age, the future me,
house & home, the required sleep, so meticulous
surrendered in making words & getting nothing
today, so this moment need not be long in making
surrender, somewhere this wind between fixtures,
crossing the street, along the horizon, my own
language a bus crowded with verse not a siren only
the tip of the future container, the tip only

Copyright © 1988 by Todd Baron

ISBN: 0-929022-02-5

ACKNOWLEDGMENTS:

Parts of this book have appeared in *Acts, Sink* and *Mirage* magazines.

O Books
5729 Clover Drive
Oakland, CA 94618

Small Press Distribution
1814 San Pablo Avenue
Berkeley, CA 94702

Inland Book Company, Inc.
22 Hemingway Avenue
East Haven, CT 06512

Bookslinger, Inc.
502 N. Prior Avenue
St. Paul, MN 55104

Other O Books
Phantom Anthems, Robert Grenier, 1986, $6.50
Dreaming Close By, Rick London, 1986, $5.00
Abjections: A Suite, Rick London, 1988, $3.50
Visible Shivers, Tom Raworth, 1987, $8.00
Catenary Odes, Ted Pearson, 1987, $5.00
O One / An Anthology, ed. Leslie Scalapino, 1988, $10.50
Dissuasion Crowds the Slow Worker, Lori Lubeski, 1988, $6.50
A Certain Slant of Sunlight, Ted Berrigan, 1988, $9.00